Máquinas maravillosas/Mighty Machines

Camiones grúa/Tow Trucks

por/by Terri DeGezelle

Traducción/Translation: Dr. Martín Luis Guzmán Ferrer
Editor Consultor/Consulting Editor: Dra. Gail Saunders-Smith

Consultor/Consultant: Jeff Hunter
Executive Director
California Tow Truck Association

Capstone *press*®

Mankato, Minnesota

Pebble Plus is published by Capstone Press,
151 Good Counsel Drive, P.O. Box 669, Mankato, Minnesota 56002.
www.capstonepress.com

1 2 3 4 5 6 11 10 09 08 07 06

Library of Congress Cataloging-in-Publication Data
DeGezelle, Terri, 1955–
    [Tow trucks. Spanish & English]
    Camiones grúas = Tow trucks/de Terri DeGezelle.
    p. cm.—(Pebble plus. Máquinas maravillosas = Pebble plus. Mighty machines)
    Includes index.
    ISBN-13: 978-0-7368-6676-7 (hardcover)
    ISBN-10: 0-7368-6676-0 (hardcover)
    1. Wreckers (Vehicles)—Juvenile literature. 2. Automobiles—Towing—Juvenile literature. I. Title:
Tow trucks. II. Title. III. Pebble plus. Máquinas maravillosas. IV. Pebble plus. Mighty machines.
    TL230.5.W74D4418 2007
    629.225—dc22   2005037464

Summary: Simple text and photographs present tow trucks, their parts, and their jobs—in both English
    and Spanish.

Editorial Credits
Martha E. H. Rustad, editor; Katy Kudela, bilingual editor; Eida del Risco, Spanish copy editor; Molly Nei,
    set designer; Ted Williams, book designer; Wanda Winch, photo researcher; Scott Thoms, photo editor

Photo Credits
Capstone Press/Karon Dubke, cover, 1, 4–5, 7, 9, 10–11, 15, 20–21; Corbis/Gunter Marx, 18–19; Peter Arnold,
Inc./Hartmut Schwarzbach, 17; UNICORN Stock Photos/Mark E. Gibson, 12–13

The author thanks Dick Longenecker, Heavy Equipment Operator, Local Union 49er, for his assistance with this
book. Pebble Plus thanks All American Towing of Mankato, Minnesota for assistance with photo shoots.

Note to Parents and Teachers

The Máquinas maravillosas/Mighty Machines set supports national standards related
to science, technology, and society. This book describes tow trucks in both English and
Spanish. The images support early readers in understanding the text. The repetition of
words and phrases helps early readers learn new words. This book also introduces early
readers to subject-specific vocabulary words, which are defined in the Glossary section.
Early readers may need assistance to read some words and to use the Table of Contents,
Glossary, Internet Sites, and Index sections of the book.

Table of Contents

Tabla de contenidos

A Tow Truck's Job

Tow trucks move
broken cars.
Tow trucks pull cars
to repair shops to be fixed.

Cómo trabajan
los camiones grúa

Los camiones grúa arrastran
a los autos averiados.
Los llevan a los talleres
para arreglarlos.

4

Parts of Tow Trucks

Tow trucks have radios.

A call on the radio tells

a tow truck driver

where help is needed.

Las partes de
los camiones grúa

Los camiones grúa tienen radios.

Una llamada por la radio le dice

al chofer del camión grúa

que alguien necesita ayuda.

radio

Tow trucks have lights that flash.

The lights warn other drivers

to be careful around tow trucks.

Los camiones grúa tienen luces intermitentes.

Estas luces son para advertirles a otros

conductores que tengan cuidado cuando

están cerca de un camión grúa.

lights/luces

Tow trucks have wheel lifts.
The wheel lift raises
the front wheels
of a broken car.

Los camiones grúa tienen un
elevador de ruedas. El elevador
de ruedas levanta las ruedas
delanteras del auto averiado.

wheel lift/elevador de ruedas

Tow trucks have booms
that stretch out.
Booms help lift big trucks
that have tipped over.

Los camiones grúa tienen un aguilón
que se estira. Los aguilones ayudan
a levantar camiones grandes que
se hayan volteado.

boom/aguilón

What Tow Trucks Do

Tow trucks carry tools

for changing tires

and fixing cars.

Qué hacen los camiones grúa

Los camiones grúa llevan

herramientas para cambiar

llantas y para arreglar los autos.

Tow trucks move broken cars
off the road.
Then traffic can pass by
on the road.

Los camiones grúa quitan
los autos averiados de
la carretera. Así el tráfico
puede avanzar.

Tow trucks pull
all kinds of vehicles.
They even tow big trucks.

Los camiones grúa pueden mover
toda clase de vehículos. Pueden
mover hasta grandes camiones.

Mighty Tow Trucks

Tow trucks help people
with broken cars.
Tow trucks are mighty machines.

Maravillosos camiones grúa

Los camiones grúa ayudan a
las personas cuando se les
descompone su auto. Los camiones
grúa son unas máquinas maravillosas.

Glossary

boom—a long metal arm that sticks out from a tow truck

flash—to blink on and off

radio—a tool, similar to a walkie-talkie, used to send and receive messages

tow—to pull something

traffic—cars and trucks moving along a road

warn—to tell people about danger

wheel lift—a metal bar on a tow truck that is shaped like the letter T; a wheel lift fits under a car's wheels and lifts them up.

Glosario

advertir—decirles a las personas que puede haber peligro

el aguilón—brazo alargado de metal que sale de los camiones grúa

el elevador de ruedas—barra de metal de los camiones grúa en forma de T; el elevador de ruedas se coloca debajo de las ruedas del auto y las levanta.

intermitente—que se prende y se apaga

el radio—herramienta similar al trasmisor portátil, o walkie-talkie, para recibir o mandar mensajes

remolcar—arrastrar un vehículo tirando de él

el tráfico—coches y camiones que avanzan por la calle

Internet Sites

FactHound offers a safe, fun way to find Internet sites related to this book. All of the sites on FactHound have been researched by our staff.

Here's how:

1. Visit *www.facthound.com*

2. Choose your grade level.

3. Type in this book ID **0736866760** for age-appropriate sites. You may also browse subjects by clicking on letters, or by clicking on pictures and words.

4. Click on the **Fetch It** button.

FactHound will fetch the best sites for you!

Index

Sitios de Internet

FactHound proporciona una manera divertida y segura de encontrar sitios de Internet relacionados con este libro. Nuestro personal ha investigado todos los sitios de FactHound. Es posible que los sitios no estén en español.

Se hace así:

1. Visita *www.facthound.com*

2. Elige tu grado escolar.

3. Introduce este código especial **0736866760** para ver sitios apropiados según tu edad, o usa una palabra relacionada con este libro para hacer una búsqueda general.

4. Haz clic en el botón **Fetch It**.

¡FactHound buscará los mejores sitios para ti!

Índice